A Note f

I dreamed up the sayings in this book late one nig because he wasn't calling, and I needed somethinc come up with almost 100 words to be made into sentences—or rather, inspirations, things to comfort and guide me through my ever-changing teenage life. I put them on cards and taped them up on the wall behind my bed, so that they would surround me in the place where I spend so much time with so many different emotions.

My girlfriends thought they were cool—"Wow Zoe," they'd say, "this is so amazing and inspiring." The boys were another story. I think they just couldn't understand the importance of these words to a teenage girl. To them they were just words.

I never in a million years planned or expected them to turn into a book, but I'm glad they have. So feel free to use them, tear them out and hang them on your walls, give them to your friends, read one every day as you get ready for school…but however you choose to use them, my hope is that they'll lead you through life, give you confidence, and forever protect you.　　　　—Zoe Stern

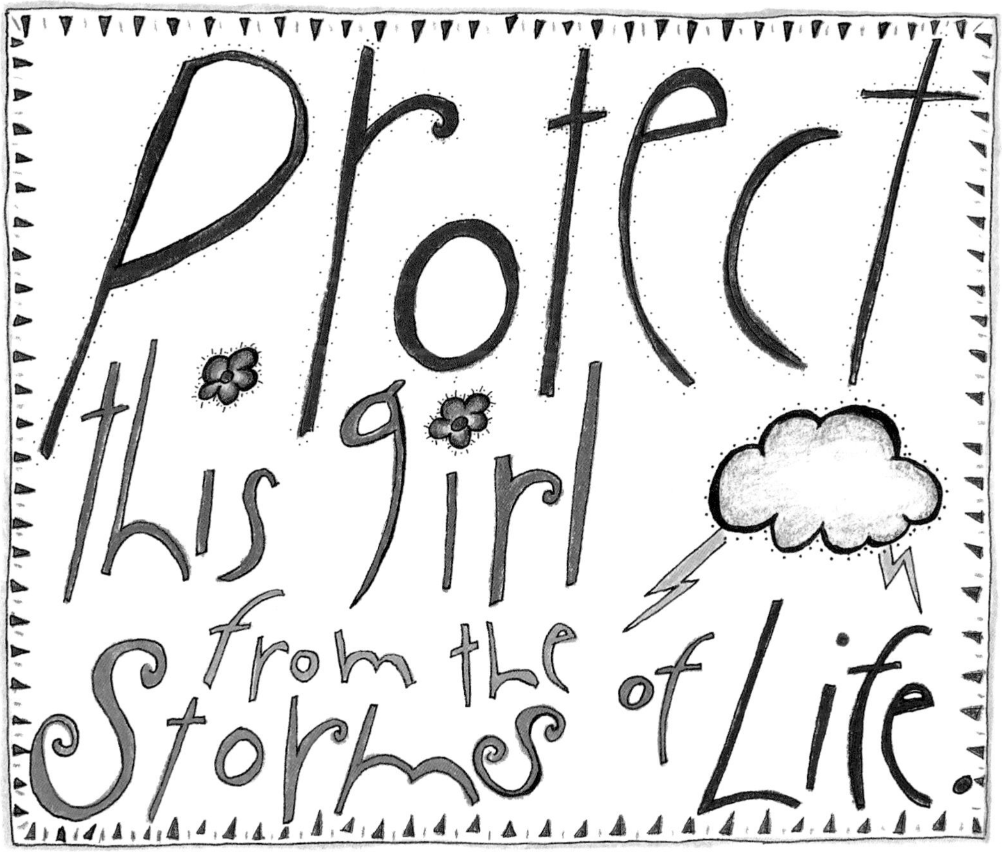
Protect this girl from the Storms of Life.

the real me is good enough.

friendship is the greatest gift

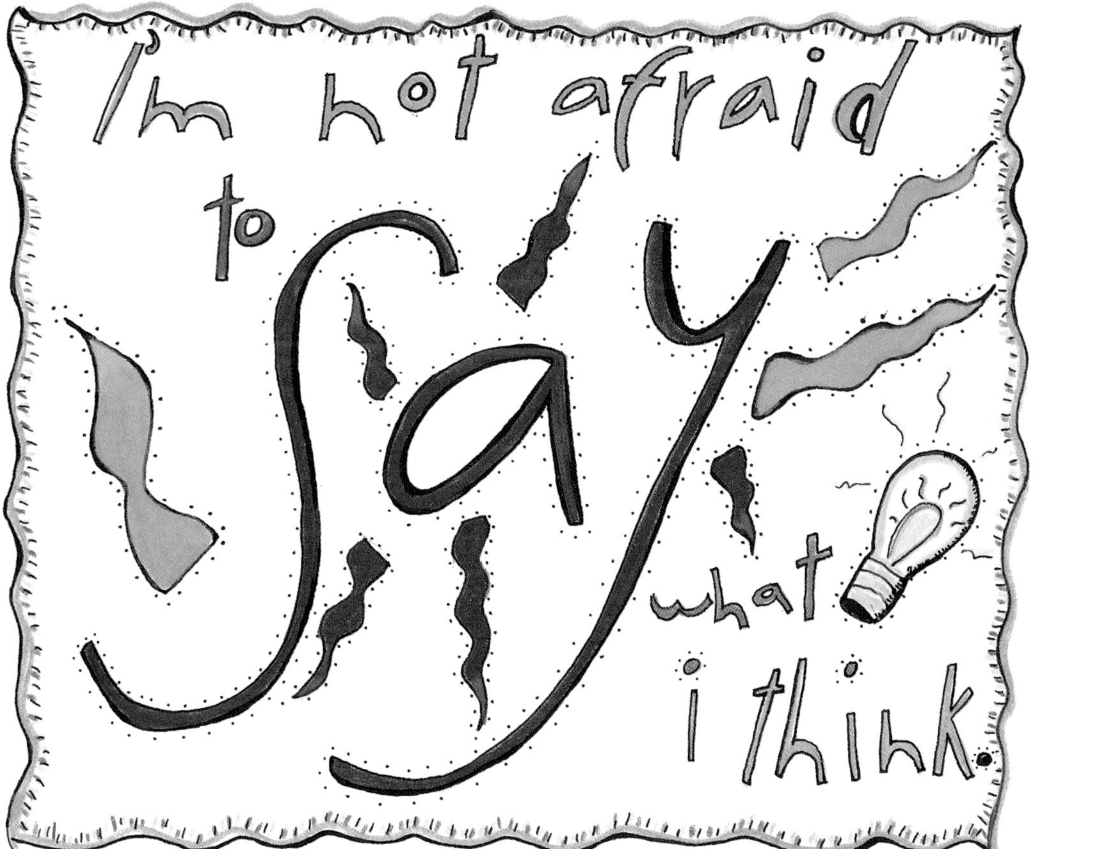
I'm not afraid
to say
what
i think.

forgiving helps mend your hurts

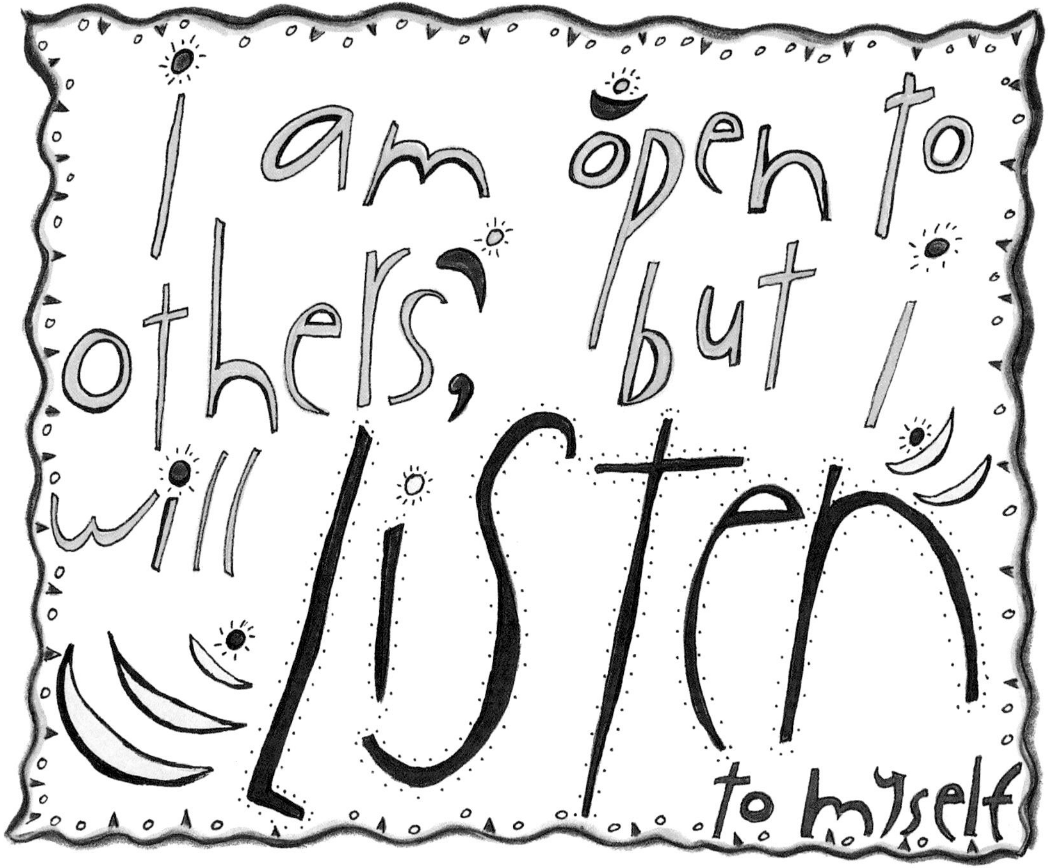
I am open to others, but I will LISTEN to myself

I can trust, but won't let anyone take advantage of me.

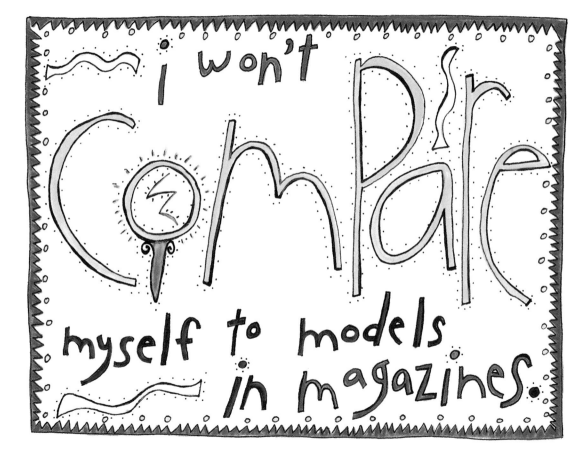

I don't need a boy to feel good about who i am.

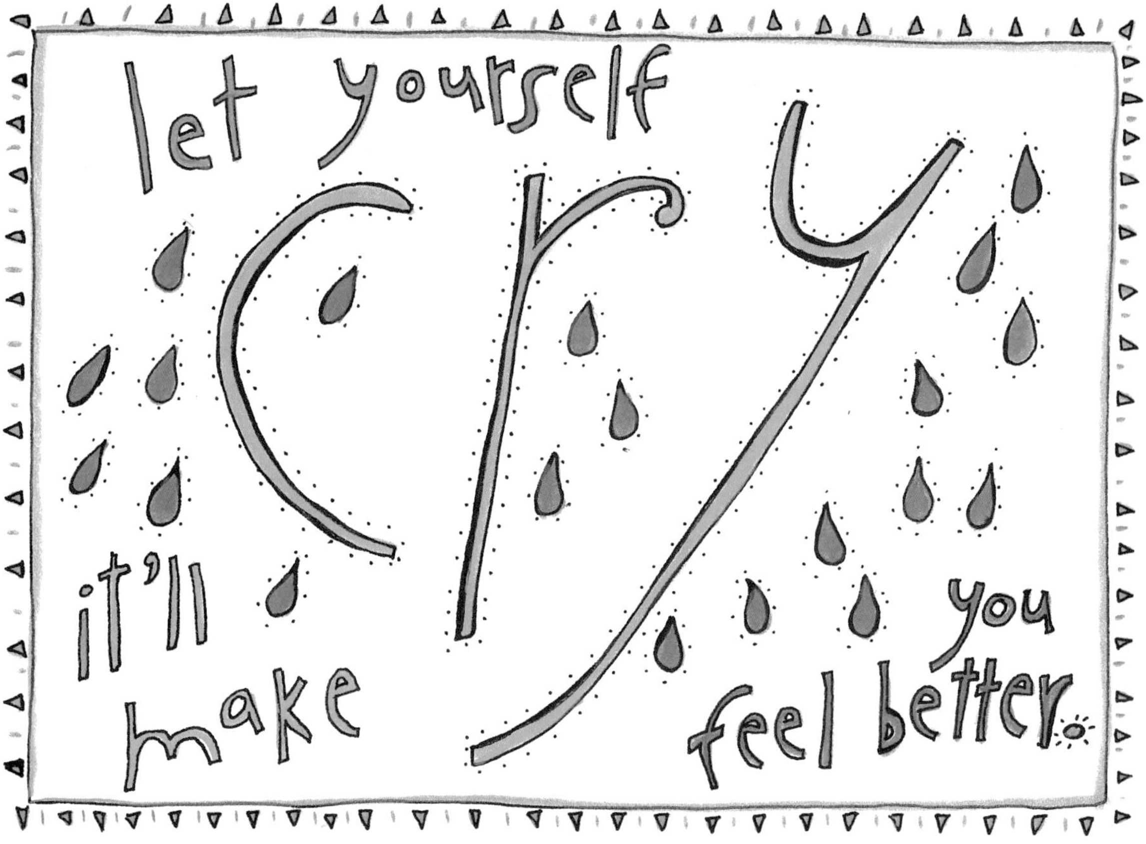
let yourself
cry
it'll make
you
feel better.

Stuffed animals are good at keeping secrets

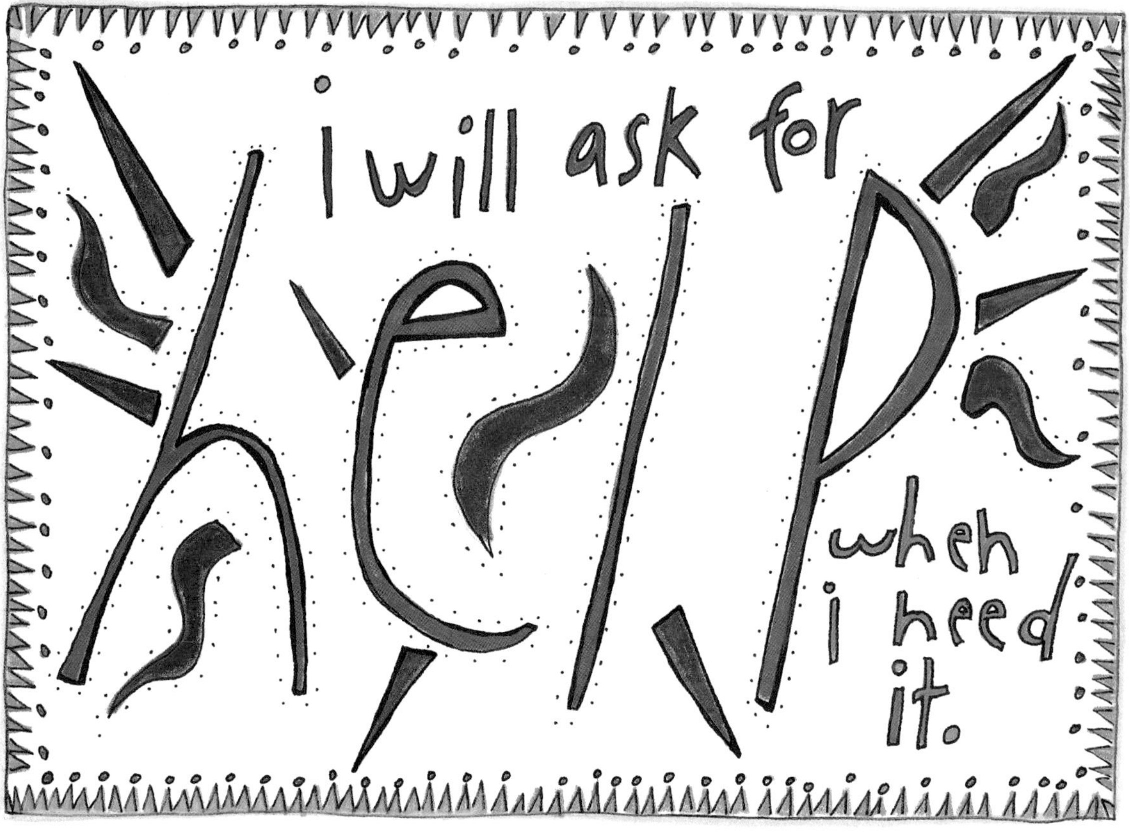
i will ask for
help
when
i need
it.

Daydreams are the things our forgot eyes to see.

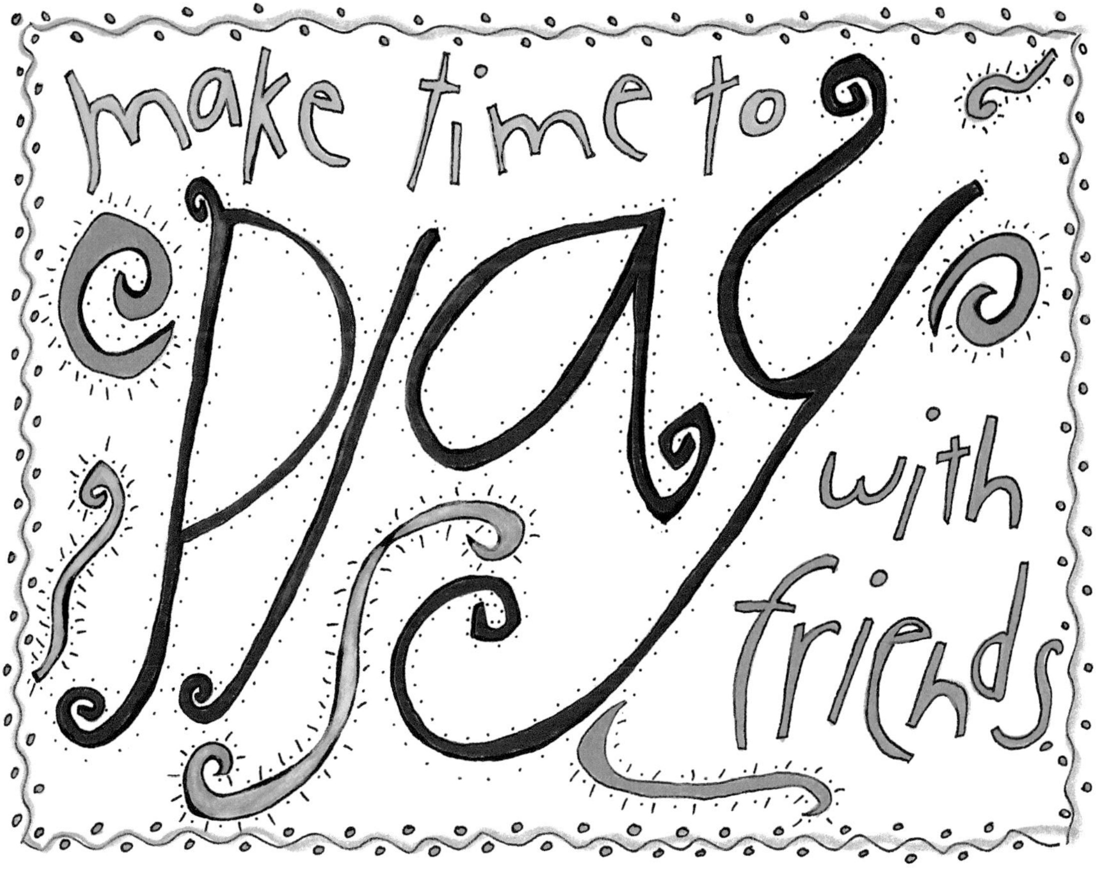
make time to
play
with
friends

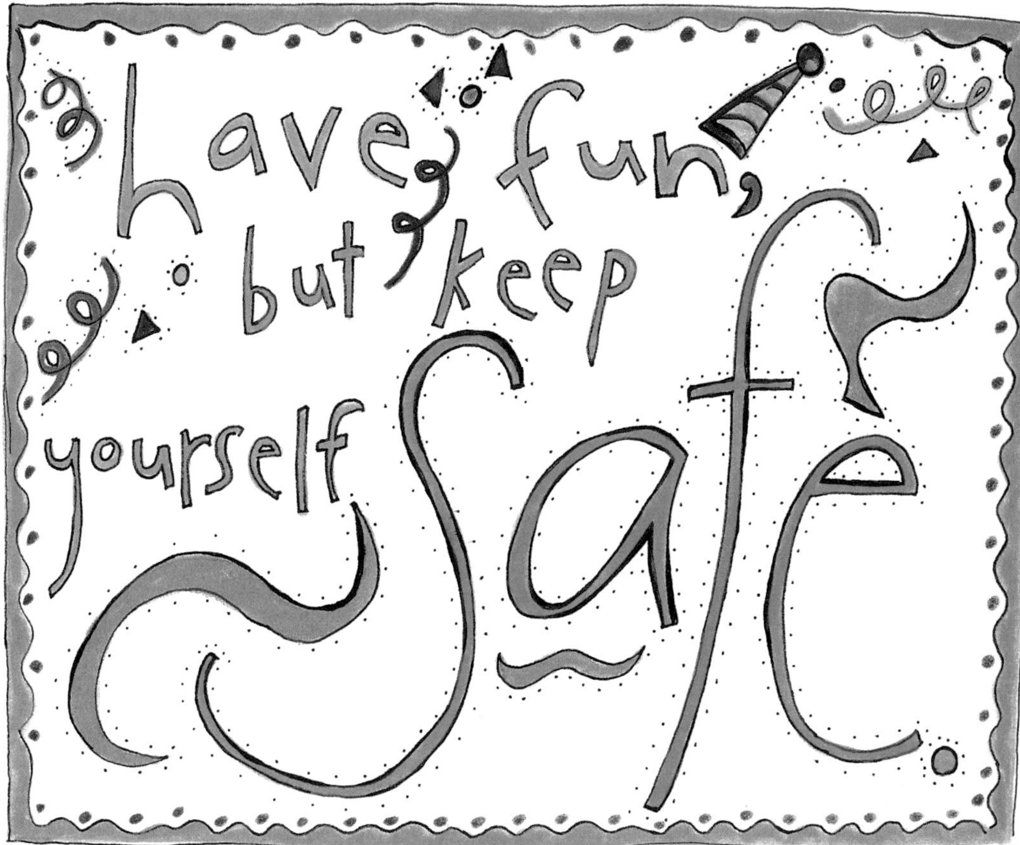

Have fun,
but keep
yourself
safe.

friends

are the people who like you the way you are

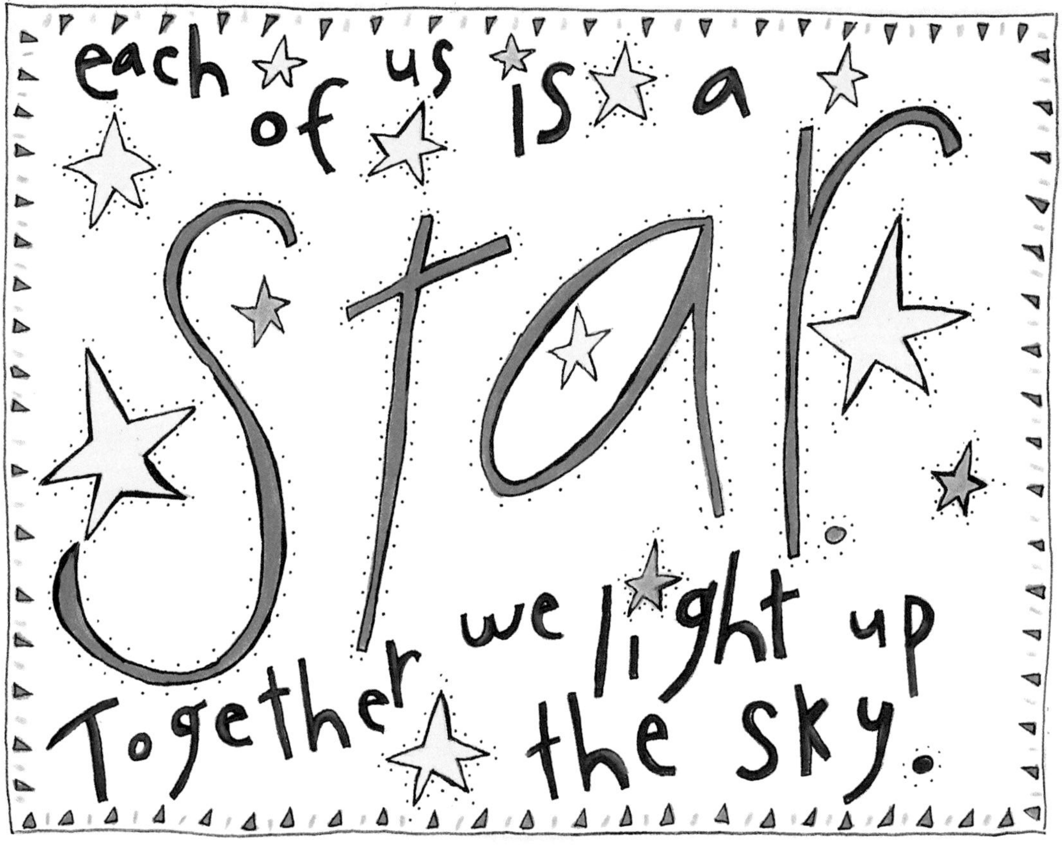
each of us is a star.
Together we light up the sky.

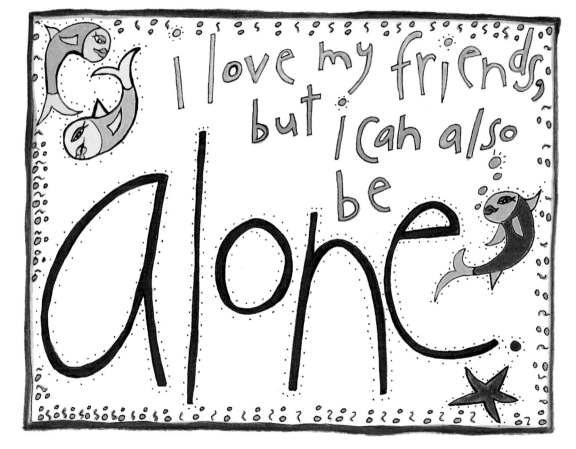

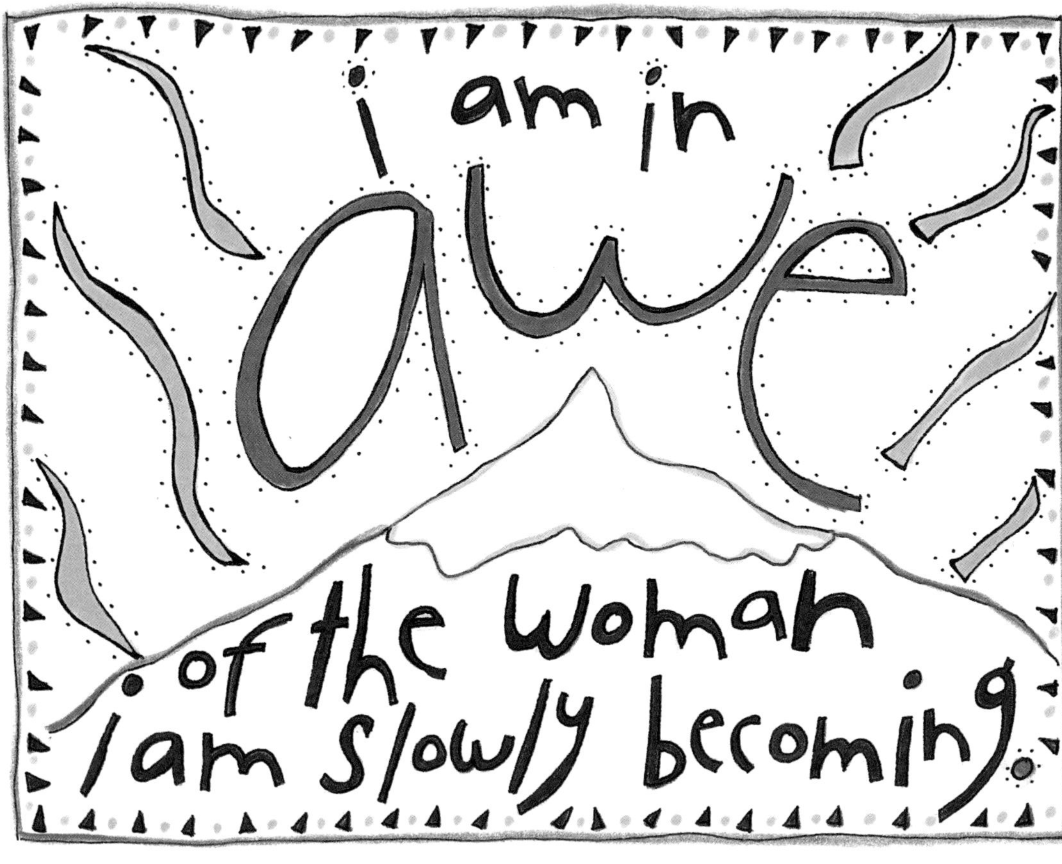
i am in
awe
of the woman
i am slowly becoming.

writing down my thoughts helps me remember who i am today.

i won't keep my anger locked up inside me.

give yourself a
present
once in a while.

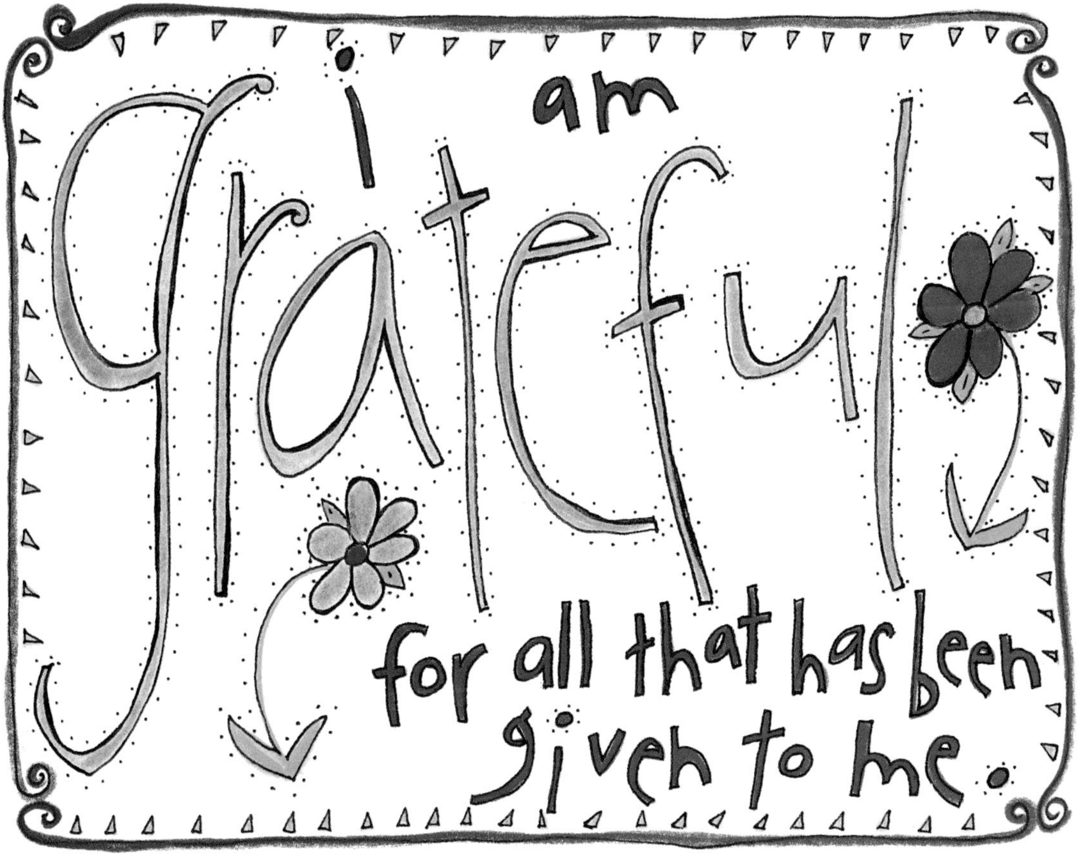
i am grateful
for all that has been given to me.

every girl is my sister